Purple Ronnie's Book of Love

Published in 1991 by Statics (London) Ltd,
41 Standard Road, London NW10 6HF.
Tel: 081-965 3327

© 1991 Giles Andreae
ISBN 1 873922 00 0

Printed in England by HPH Print Ltd.,
8 Gorst Road, London NW10 6LE.

Words by Giles Andreae
and Simon Andreae

Pictures by Janet Cronin
and Giles Andreae

Contents

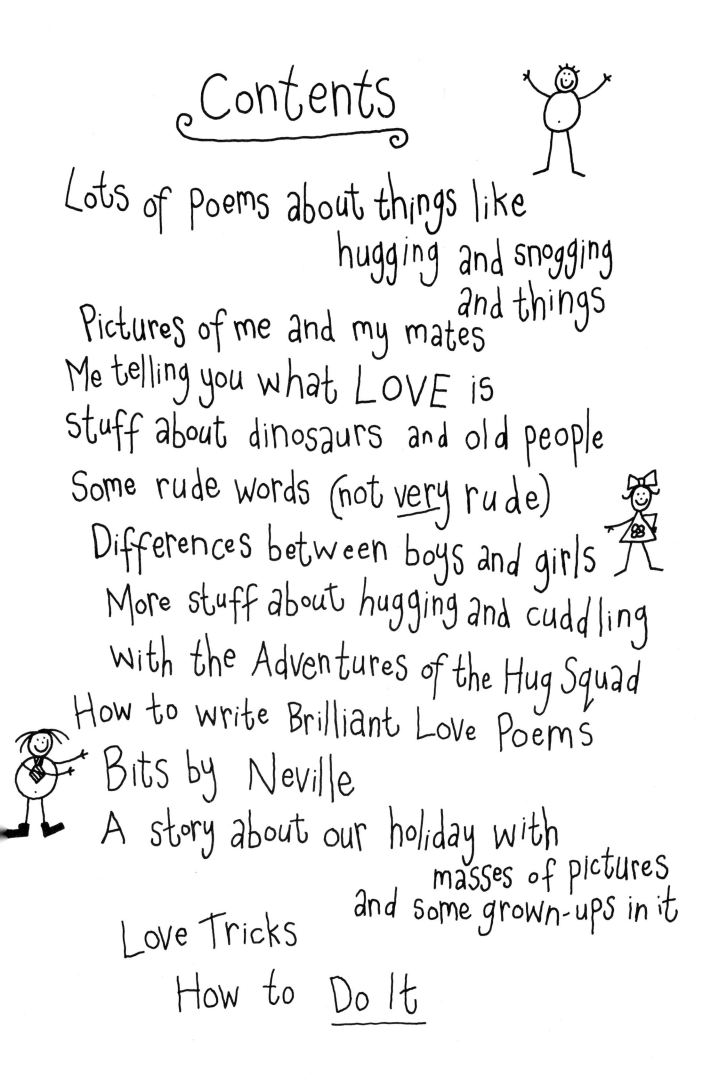

What is Love?

It must be sort of squidgey
Like a bouncy rubber ball
Cos I know that when you fall in it
It doesn't hurt at all

I know that people make it
But they never tell me where
And I think that there's a funny tribe
Who rub it in their hair

I wonder what it looks like
I've heard it's splendid stuff
I suppose it's sort of furry
Like my tummy button fluff

piece of love

love

dance

Jammy Bun Poem 1

When I think of Jammy Buns
I rush off to the shop
And say I want a million please
Then scoff them till I pop

wobble

me
about
to blow
up

→ Mr BunMan

1
LOVE
Jammy
Buns
BUT
I do not
want to
SNOG
Them

.P.R.

Jammy Bun Poem 2

Neville is a splendid chap
Oh crikey he's so nice
I'd like to buy a Jammy bun
And offer him a slice

titchy piece of Jammy bun

I
LOVE
my
friends
even
Neville

.P.R.

Jammy Bun Poem 3

My tummy starts to jump around
And then my brain goes swirlie
But not because of Jammy Buns
But cos I'm with my girlie

whizz
swirl

skip
gambol
no buns

I LOVE my girlie so much I don't even THINK of Jammy Buns when I'm with her. This is the kind of LOVE that makes you dance and skip (even if you're a boy) and do all sorts of silly things - sometimes even IT

Make sure you give things the right kind
of LOVE or else
you might get in
a frightful muddle
and start DOING IT
with a Jammy Bun

I love you
I love you...
and I want to
have your babies

Yikes!

?

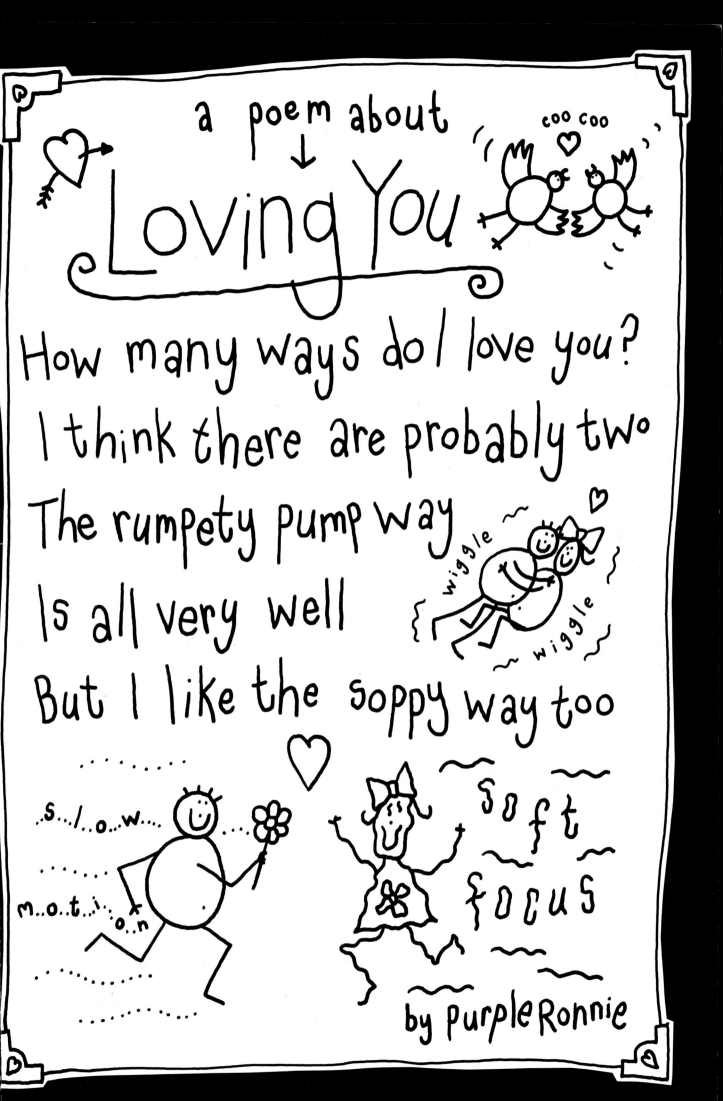

HOW LOVE WAS INVENTED

Millions of years ago before love was invented, the only creatures on earth were <u>dinosaurs</u>. They were horrid warty animals with lumps and bumps and scales and spikes and scarey names like Smellydactyl and Bottisaurus.

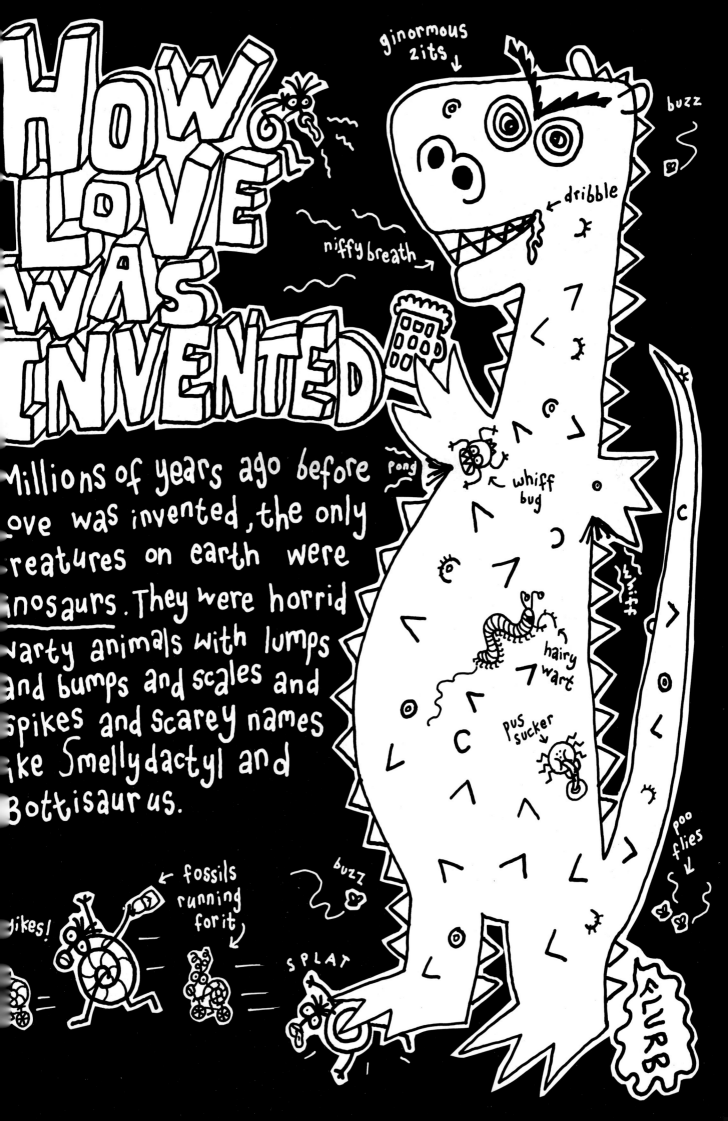

ginormous zits ↓

buzz

← dribble

niffy breath →

pong

← whiff bug

hairy wart

pus sucker ↓

← fossils running for it

yikes!

buzz

SPLAT

poo flies ↓

FLURB

All the dinosaurs soon died off because they never wanted to make babies with eachother, so when it came to thinking up PEOPLE God had already learnt some very important lessons

God needed something that would make people like the things he'd invented like trees and beer and sweets and discos

munch munch

you're so big and green and wonderful

L♥B

BUT MOST OF ALL THEY HAD TO LIKE EACHOTHER

Each person had to specially like someone different and want to do RUDE THINGS with them so the new-style people would never die out like the old and ugly dinosaurs

go for it purp

honestly he likes you!

The thing he invented had to be friendly and cuddly so people would want to play with it and muck around with it and share it out with all their mates

it had to start tiny so it could fit into all the different people whatever size or shape. they were

itch itch

But when it was there it had to be able to grow and grow and grow until the whole world was full of it and people would go all WONKY and nearly BLOW UP with it

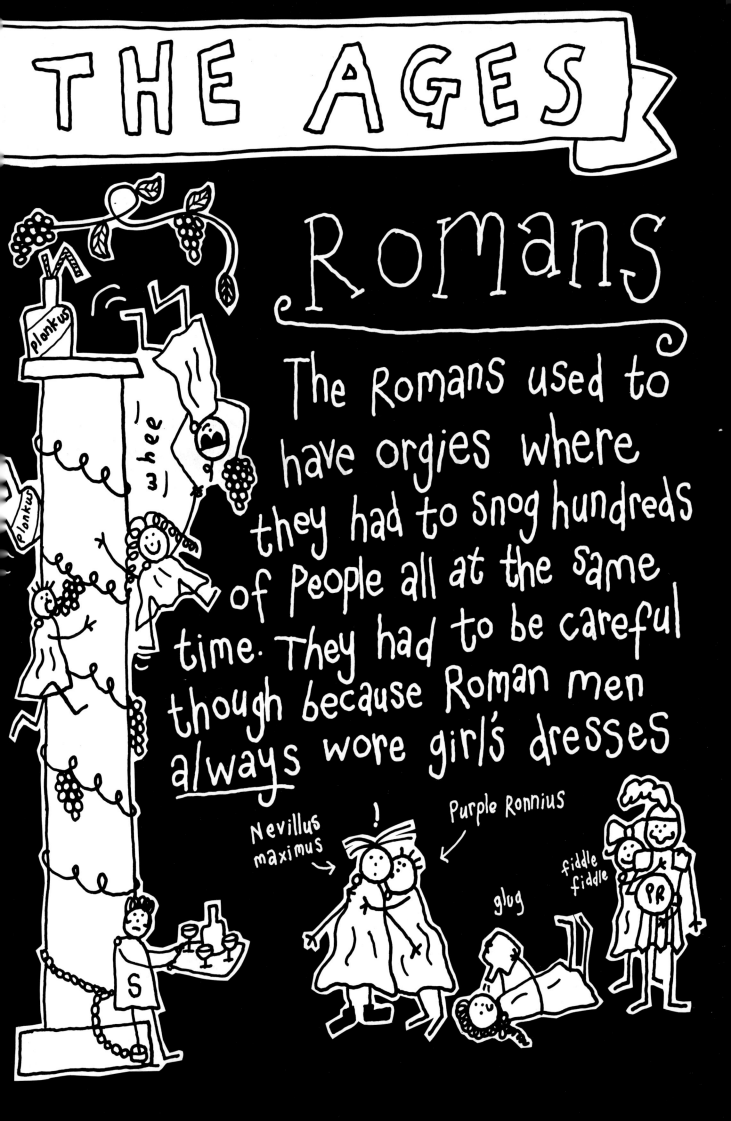

Middle Ages

Pants were invented in the middle ages, but they were made out of scratchy sacks which meant that no-one wanted to DO IT because their bits were too sore

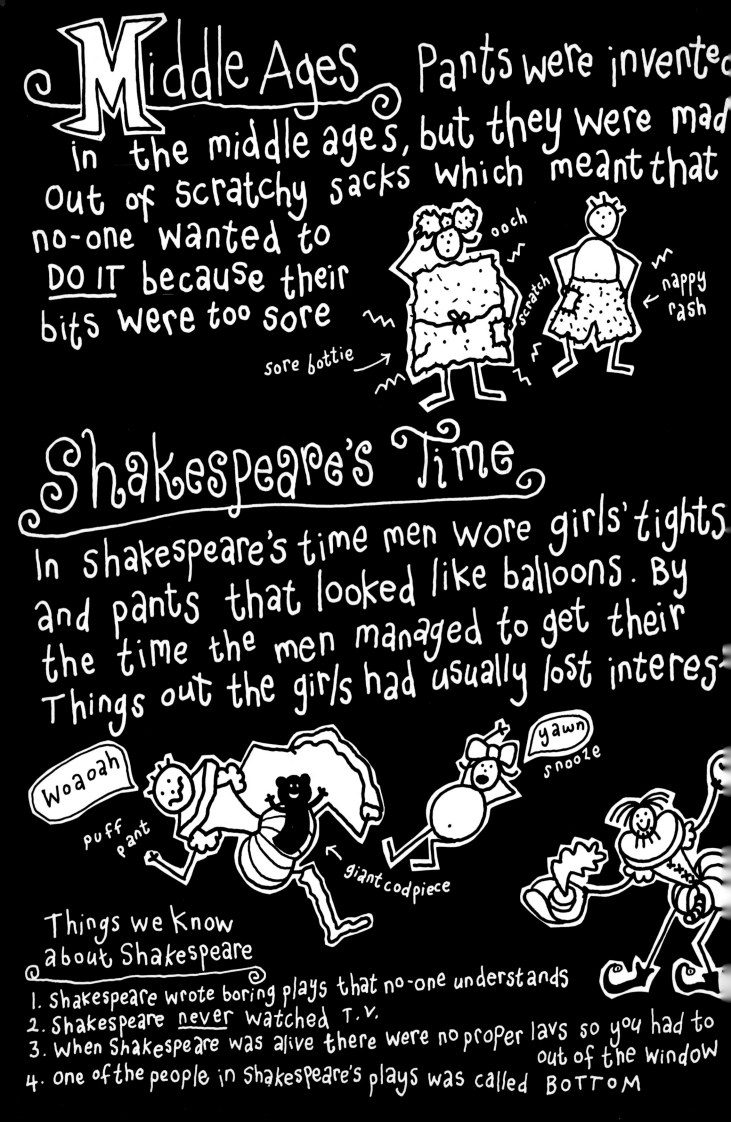

ooch

scratch

nappy rash

sore bottie →

Shakespeare's Time

In shakespeare's time men wore girls' tights and pants that looked like balloons. By the time the men managed to get their Things out the girls had usually lost interes

Woaoah

puff pant

giant codpiece →

yawn

snooze

Things we know about Shakespeare

1. Shakespeare wrote boring plays that no-one understands
2. Shakespeare <u>never</u> watched T.V.
3. When Shakespeare was alive there were no proper lavs so you had to out of the window
4. one of the people in Shakespeare's plays was called BOTTOM

a poem about a →

Smashing Mate

You're chocolate cake
and soft ice cream
Piled high upon my plate
You're a double jelly
sandwich dream
My splendid smashing mate

by
Purple
Ronnie

THE WORDS OF LOVE

Love Handles

Love handles are on the sides of girls' bottoms and you must only pull them when the girl wants to have a baby.
The baby says to its Mum "Let me out" so the doctor pulls the girls handles and the baby comes flying out

special baby doctor →

z o i n g

wheee

Love Juice

Love juice is a potion you must drink if you want to be good at love
You make it up from ground up pieces of love and milk

ground LOVE

)) whizz

splurge

MILK

FOR SALE
Love juice
2P a bottle

Love Machine

The love machine is a special invention for people who don't have anyone to give them any love. When you turn it on two arms come out and put you in a ginormous cuddle until you're completely bursting with love

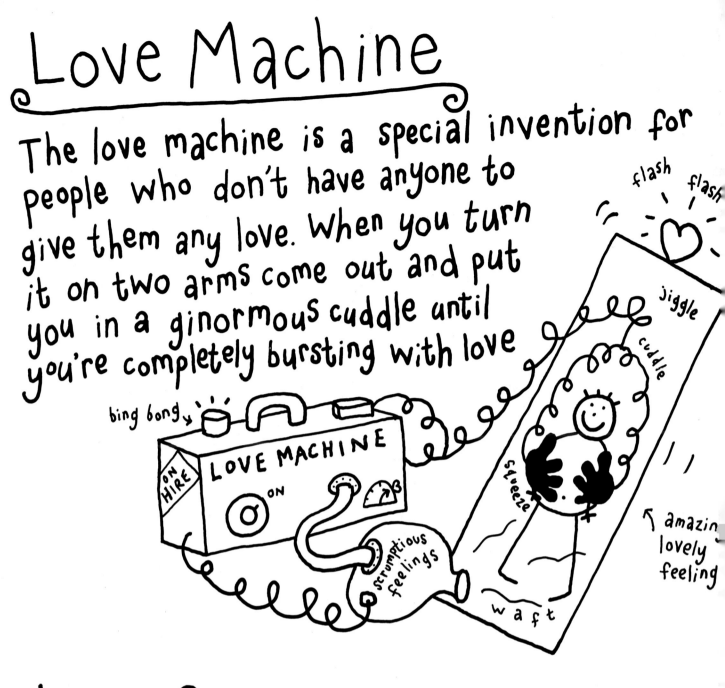

bing bong
LOVE MACHINE
ON HIRE
ON
scrumptious feelings
flash flash
jiggle
cuddle
squeeze
← amazin lovely feeling
waft

Love Bug

The love bug is a disease that makes you very poorly and makes all your love leak out. If you get it you must wrap yourself up in a big blanket to try and sto all the love escaping

little bits of love leaking out
← poorly
love doctor →

Love Tangle

A love tangle is when you love someone so much that all your feelings for them get completely tangled up

Love Nest

A love nest is a place that rich men build where girls can go to lay their eggs if they haven't got enough money for their own house

a poem about

Girls

When I ask girls for a date
They always seem to worry
What is wrong with a jug of ale
And a steaming plate of curry?

by Purple Ronnie

CUDDLING MATCHES

At Cuddling Matches all the men dress up in shorts and get into two gangs

There is one man who skips and dances and puts his hands up.
He is the Snuggle Judge who is called the referee.
When he blows his whistle the gangs run towards him and get ready to have a mass Snuggle. They do this by bending over and holding onto eachother's pants

phreep

grunt

squidge

oof!

Someone tries to put a ball into the snuggle but the men are having such a cosy time that they just scrape it out of the way

The players then take it in turns to run around and make eachother fall over by hugging their legs

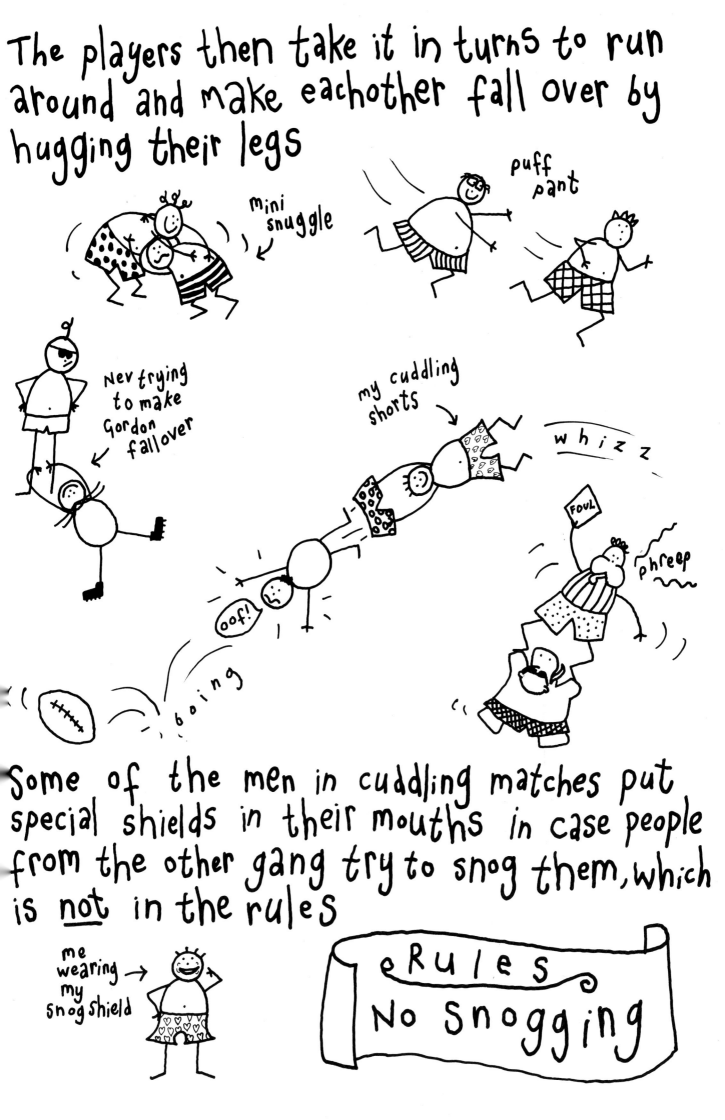

mini snuggle

puff pant

Nev trying to make Gordon fallover

my cuddling shorts

whizz

FOUL

phreep

oof!

boing

Some of the men in cuddling matches put special shields in their mouths in case people from the other gang try to snog them, which is **not** in the rules

me wearing my snog shield →

RULES
No snogging

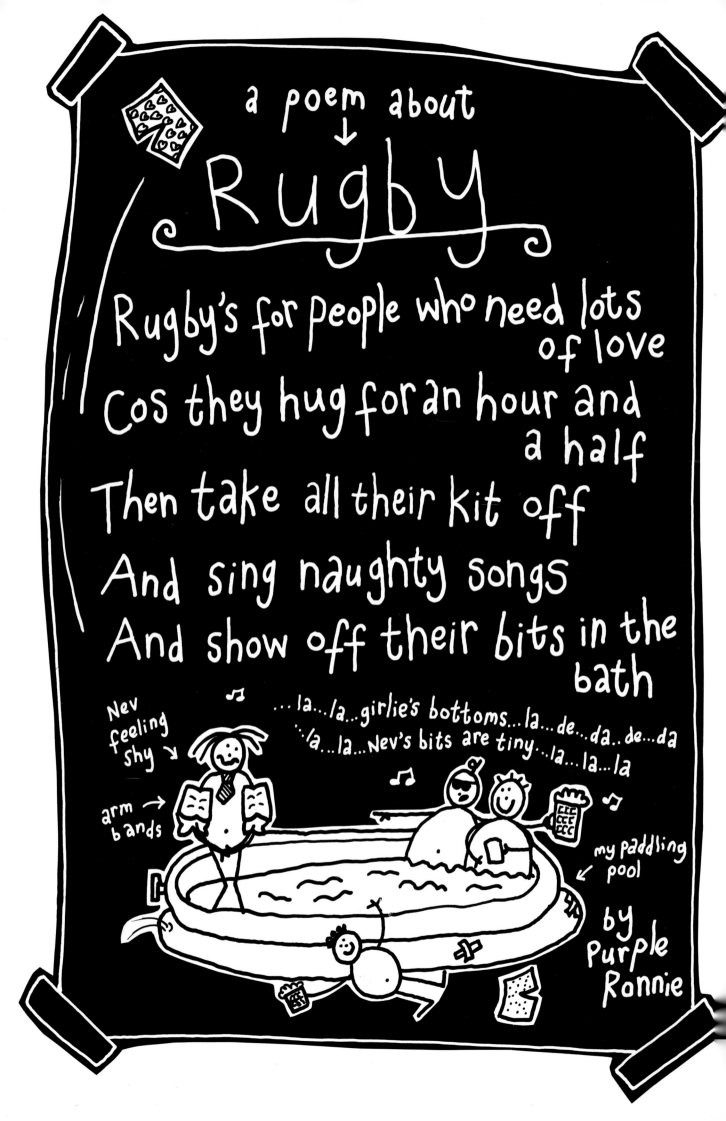

a poem about

Men's Bits

Men's bits sometimes look like bananas
And sometimes like shrivelled up grapes
But however they try
They just can't deny
That they come in the silliest shapes

by Purple Ronnie

Hugging

" "

Ever since people were invented they have spent most of their time thinking up all sorts of brainy words so they can talk to eachother about incredibly grown-up things and tell eachother how amazingly clever they are

we'll have to scrunge the wibblesnack with a tickling hose and scragglepoop the bottyhiss with a double grundle

it's either that or a full dingleslip to the trouserpipe

24 hour dingle-slip Job 20p

hiss

The problem with words is that they are useless when you want to tell people how you're feeling and talk about what's going on INSIDE YOU

x-ray machine

a poem about
My Own Little Way

I sometimes get rather
embarrassed
And don't always know what
to say
When it comes to expressing
my feelings
But I try in my own little way

I sort of...well... it's just that... well

shuffle
shuffle

THE ONLY LANGUAGE PEOPLE CAN REALLY USE TO SAY IMPORTANT THINGS IS THE LANGUAGE OF HUGGING

hug master →

Hug

A hug is the deepest way there is for one person to say something to another. It is given standing very still with the eyes closed. You hold eachother so tightly that your feelings are squodged together into one ginormous feeling of L O V E L I N E S S

Cuddle

A cuddle is shared between 2 people who want to say the same thing to eachother. You can cuddle while:

<u>sitting</u>   or   <u>lying down</u>

jiggle   jiggle

you hold eachother more loosely than in a hug, and jiggle around until your feelings are nicely shaken about and mixed together

YOU ALWAYS COME OUT OF A CUDDLE <u>SMILING</u>

Snuggle

A snuggle is used mainly for warmth and comfort and can ONLY be had lying down

Snuggling is done under warm blankets or in little hidey holes

It is wet nosed and gentle and is good at keeping MONSTERS away

yikes!

Huggle

A huggle is only used by people who are bubbling over with happiness. You can huggle while dancing, jumping, or skipping down the street. Huggles can say ANYTHING YOU LIKE. You can give crazy huggles and you can even huggle yourself!

huggle crazy

ee!

a Snuggley Poem

I'd like to be a hamster

that's me

Or a hedgehog or a shrew

And go into my hidey hole

To snuggle up with you

us having a
snuggley time

DO NOT
DISTURB

goose-
berry

HIDEY
HOLE →

by Purple Ronnie

a recipe for Love Pie

by Purple Ronay

Take a pint of tickle juice
And whisk it till it's thick
Pick a crop of cuddle fruit
And crush them with a stick

♥

Nibble eighteen earlobes
As gently as you can
Then grate a little botty kiss
And put it in the pan

♥

Dip a snog in snuggle sauce
And let it rest a while
Then soak it in hug marinade
and season with a smile

♥

Add a pinch of happy spice
Grown in huggle town
And bake it in the oven
Till it comes out
golden brown

a poem about

Smiley Inside

Love makes you feel all cuddly
                          and warm
Love makes your tongue get all
                                  tied
It makes you go wobbly
And weak at the knees
And all sort of smiley inside

by
Purple
Ronnie

a poem about

Being in Love

Whenever I'm with you
My heart starts to thump
And I come over wonky and flustered
I try to stay calm
But pour milk on my toast
And butter my coffee with
mustard

me so
← in Love

by
Purple
Ronnie

How to Write a _{Brilliant} Love Poem

Writing Love Poems is great because you can sit down all by yourself and tell someone exactly how you feel about them without having to say it out loud and getting your feelings tangled and all your words jumbled up

compare these 2 poems

Crikey I love you to pieces
My heart wants to jump up and shout
Let's walk through the flowers
And huggle for hours
And let all our loveliness out

Love Poem 1

Crikey your bits are ginormous
I'd love to get into your knicks
Forget soppy flowers
Let's do it for hours
I do that with all of my chicks

Yikes! help!

Love Poem 2

Rude Police

phreep

CHUCK

come here baby!

Most people would prefer to be sent **Love Poem 1**. This is because in **Love Poem 2** I have broken all the rules. You must stick to the rules when you write Love poems or people will not love you for very long

The Rules

<u>DO NOT</u> tell someone they've got huge bits (unless he's a man)

<u>DO</u> use soppy words

<u>DO NOT</u> tell someone you're desperate to DO IT

<u>DO</u> tell them they're smashing to be with

<u>DO NOT</u> tell someone you DO IT with lots of other people

<u>DO</u> talk about cuddly feelings

<u>DO NOT</u> talk about girls' pants

This is a story that Neville wrote when he was small. The teacher said it sounded like a nice place and she would like to go there too. Neville said he couldn't remember where it was

← Nev being small

The Tru Story of NEVILLE in the LAnd of Luv

Wen i went to this lAnd orl the peepl sed i cood be in ther gang and the gels did not laf at mi shortz and corl me weedi. We Playd a game Wer you kisz the gels Nicly anD say orl tHE things you luv aBouT the otHer persin and sum of the PeePls Did say they luv mi Hairstyl and suM Did lik mi SHorts

We went To Tea with the King hoo livd in a giafmas gynarms grATE Big palis and wos veri rich and givD us massis of SWEETS but he had no LAv paper so ORL the peepls Did wip ther BOTTOMS with thEr hands

milyons of SWEETS

The king thort i wos grate becoz i told him the jok of DUNNER PLOP and he Did Laf for agiz

Afterwerds orl the MEN of the Land Wontid to mari the PRINCESZ and the KiNg Sed you must hav a VOT to see hoo is the most hansm and brave Persin iN the land and orl of the LaDis Sed NEVILLE NEVILLE

↑ orl the Ladis charging at me

SPESHLY the PRINCESS sed i wos Smashing anD wen we got mariD the king Mad a Speech and Sed i can be thE next KiNg of this land after he is Ded and Hav orl his munee and orl the PEEpls clapt and staid up LAt to muk around with US

THE END

a poem about

Love

Love,
When we're SNOGGING
I'd like to crumble
Biscuits in your hair

crumble
crumble

snogging

by Purple
Ronnie

BICS

a poem about
Kissing

Some kisses last for just seconds
They're gentle and go on the cheeks
But I like the ones you put right on the lips
That can go on for 2 or 3 weeks

a poem about
Marathon Snoggers

Keep out of the way of the marathon snoggers
Who don't need to come up for breath
They go for the record each time that they start
And they sometimes snog people to death

a poem about

Soggy Ones

me hiding

Uncles and aunts give you this kind of Kiss
When they squeeze you all up in a bunch
And plant a great soggy one
Right on your lips
And look like they'll eat you for lunch

slurp
hoover

my Auntie Phil →

Yummy!

a poem about a

Greedy Kiss

chase me
chase me

Greedy people seem to think
It's scrumpelicious fun
To munch your neck and bite your ears
And snog off half your tongue

snog
munch

← oooch!

me feeling cheesed off

a poem about a

Squodgey Kiss

This is the kiss your Mum sometimes gives
If you're lonely or stuck in a rut
She wraps you all up in a lovely big hug
And then squodges one right on your nut

squodge

← much better

a poem about

Snogging

← true love

It's funny how us people
Show our love by touching tongues
But at least we're not all doggies
Or we'd sniff eachother's bums!

down boy!

sniff sniff

Here is a trick so that girls will let you feel their wibbly-wobbly bits

This is a brilliant trick to say if you want to snog someone. You can find out if they want to snog you and if they don't you get away without looking silly ↴

saying things the other way round can often get you out of trouble but remember not to try this trick if you want to say things like
☆ Can I tickle your bits? or
☆ Can I fiddle with your parts?
as they are sometimes ruder the other way round

Knobs and Switches

Girls have knobs under their jersies that you have to twist and a special switch to turn on the electricity in their pants

crackle

off on

buzz

← girls' pants

Oooh

If you forget about these you might as well go home because girls have to be turned on properly to DO IT

The G-Spot

The G-Spot was discovered five years ago by an incredibly brainy scientist. It is very small and can only be seen with a special microscope. If you find it you must not press too hard or it might explode and make a terrible mess

professor Rude ↓

ooohh aaahh

Gadgets

It is always best to use protection but you must make sure you get the right sort

←wrong

Sometimes you can use special love gadgets and put on saucy pants

INSTRUCTIONS

buzz

our amazing love gadgets

Actually Doing IT

It is polite to ask the girl first if you can DO IT with her and if she says yes please you must close your eyes while she takes off her clothes.

can I DO IT with you?

yes please

wriggle

squeal!

snog

snuggle

Then you must snuggle up very close together and wriggle and snog and squeal all at the same time. DO NOT laugh at the girl's bosoms or wobble them around because bosoms are not funny - they are AMAZING

After Doing IT

You must not stop DOING IT until the girl says you can, then you must hug the girl and tell her she is smashing for ages. Do not punch the girl if she shores

no biffing

Things not to say after DOING IT
1. Thanks
2. Do you want some money?
3. can I go to the toilet now?

Love

If you want to snuggle, wriggle, squeal, snog and hug with the girl all the time then you are probably feeling love. Do not worry about this because LOVE IS THE MOST AMAZING THING THAT HAS EVER BEEN INVENTED

a poem about

Falling in Love

Sing about it
Shout about it
Jump up and down
And tell all the people about it
Love
Love
Love
That's what it is
HOORAY!

by Purple
Ronnie

Bye
Bye